Levi Strauss

by Lucia Raatma

Compass Point Early Biographies

Content Adviser: Nancy Lemke, California Historian and Author,
Bonita, California

Thank you to Lynn Downey, Levi Strauss & Co. Historian,
and Stacia Fink, Levi Strauss & Co. Archivist,
San Francisco, California

Reading Adviser: Dr. Linda D. Labbo,
Department of Reading Education, College of Education,
The University of Georgia

COMPASS POINT BOOKS
Minneapolis, Minnesota

Compass Point Books
3109 West 50th Street, #115
Minneapolis, MN 55410

Visit Compass Point Books on the Internet at *www.compasspointbooks.com*
or e-mail your request to *custserv@compasspointbooks.com*

Photographs ©: San Francisco History Center, San Francisco Public Library, cover, 15, 17, 20, 23, 24;
Levi Strauss & Co. Archives, 4, 16, 19; Courtesy of Levi Strauss Museum, Buttenheim, Germany, 7, 26;
Corbis, 8, 11; Photri-Microstock, 9; Stock Montage, Inc., 10; North Wind Picture Archives, 12;
Hulton/Archive by Getty Images, 13, 14; AP/Wide World Photos, Vintage Designs Limited, 18;
Library of Congress, 21; James Leynse/Corbis SABA, 27.

Editor: Christianne C. Jones
Photo Researcher: Marcie C. Spence
Designer/Page Production: Bradfordesign, Inc./Les Tranby

Library of Congress Cataloging-in-Publication Data
Raatma, Lucia.
    Levi Strauss / by Lucia Raatma.
        p. cm. — (Compass Point early biographies)
Summary: Briefly introduces the life of Levi Strauss, a Bavarian Jew who immigrated to the United
States in 1847 and became a very successful businessman and philanthropist after inventing blue jeans.
Includes bibliographical references and index.
ISBN 0-7565-0568-2 (hardcover)
1. Strauss, Levi, 1829-1902—Juvenile literature. 2. Businessmen—United States—Biography—
    Juvenile literature. 3. Clothing trade—United States—History—Juvenile literature. 4. Jeans
    (Clothing)—History—Juvenile literature. 5. Levi Strauss and Company—History—Juvenile
    literature. [1. Strauss, Levi, 1829-1902. 2. Businesspeople. 3. Clothing trade. 4. Levi Strauss
    and Company—History.] I. Title. II. Series.
        HD9940.U4S7976 2004
        338.7'687'092—dc22   2003012283

Table of Contents

*NOTE: In this book, words that are defined in the glossary are in **bold** the first time they appear in the text.*

The Famous Red Tab

Levi Strauss is the inventor of blue jeans. The famous red tab on Levi's® jeans bears his name, and so does the major clothing company—Levi Strauss & Co. He was a hard-working, honest, and generous man. He was also a caring family man.

Although people were already wearing denim pants in the 1800s, Levi Strauss and Jacob Davis made them stronger and more durable by adding **rivets**. This was the birth of jeans. Today, Levi's® jeans are one of the most popular clothing items in the world.

◄ Levi Strauss in later years

Coming to the United States

Levi Strauss wasn't always called Levi. He was born Loeb Strauss on February 26, 1829, in Buttenheim, Bavaria. Loeb Strauss became Levi Strauss when his family moved to the United States.

Levi's parents, Hirsch and Rebecca Strauss, did their best to raise their family. Hirsch sold dry goods to make money.

However, life in Bavaria was tough for the Strauss family because they were Jewish. The Bavarian government treated Jewish people differently. Jewish people could live only on certain streets and had to pay special taxes.

Levi's birth house in Buttenheim was turned into the Levi Strauss Museum. Bavaria is now part of Germany.

A young peddler with his
heavy pack of dry goods

When Levi was only a teenager, Hirsch Strauss died from **tuberculosis**. Levi and his brothers worked as **peddlers** to support the family. They walked from house to house, carrying heavy packs full of dry goods to sell.

In 1847, Levi and his mother and sisters decided to **immigrate** to the United States. They had heard that the United States was a

Millions of immigrants made their way
to North America on crowded ships. ➤

place where everyone was treated fairly. They were going to join Levi's brothers, Jonas and Louis, who already lived in New York City. Getting to New York meant surviving a long trip across the Atlantic Ocean on a ship. The ship was crowded and dirty, but Levi and his family looked forward to a better life.

Making a Living

The Strauss family worked hard to make a living in New York City. Levi's brothers had a wholesale dry goods business

Hundreds of immigrants applied to become U.S. citizens every day.

called J. Strauss Brothers & Co. They sold different items to small retail stores.

In January 1853, Levi became a U.S. citizen. Around that same time, he moved from New York City to San Francisco. However, people could not travel by train all the way

◀ Peddlers filled the streets of New York City in the mid-1800s.

Despite the long trip, thousands of people headed to California in the mid-1800s.

to the West Coast, and airplanes had not been invented yet. Levi made another journey by ship. It was a long trip, but he knew he'd done the right thing when he arrived in California.

Miners panning for gold in the 1850s ➤

Life in San Francisco

California was an exciting place in the 1850s. The gold rush had started a few years before. Crowds of people came to the state hoping to find gold and strike it rich. Even if they didn't find gold, many people settled in California. They started new businesses or farmed the rich soil.

San Francisco around 1855

Once in San Francisco, Strauss established his own wholesale dry goods business. Strauss made a living by selling cloth, thread, and other items to small stores around California. In 1863, he named his company Levi Strauss & Co. He moved his business to a large building on Battery Street in San Francisco.

Levi Strauss & Co. building on Battery Street in 1880

The Blue Jeans Man

In 1872, Strauss got
an interesting letter
from Jacob Davis.
Davis was a **tailor**
in Reno, Nevada.
He was a good

Jacob Davis

client of Levi's. Davis had a customer who
complained that the pockets on his denim pants
always ripped. Davis tried making the seams
around the pockets stronger by attaching little
copper rivets. The rivets worked, and Davis sent
a letter to Levi explaining his new idea.

16

Strauss liked the idea. In 1873, the two men received a **patent** for the riveted denim pants. Miners loved the sturdy pants, as did cowboys. Levi's pants became popular, and Strauss soon expanded his business. He opened factories to produce the pants. Davis moved to San Francisco to work with Strauss.

As time went by, other companies made denim pants. To let people know

An employee at a Levi's factory works on a new pair of jeans.

which pants were Levi's® jeans, the company put **trademarks** on many of the jeans' unique features. The stitching on the rear pockets was one of those trademarks. The leather patch with the two horses was also trademarked. In 1890, the original pants style was named 501. The red tab went on Levi's products in 1936. All of these items are trademarked and make Levi's® jeans truly original.

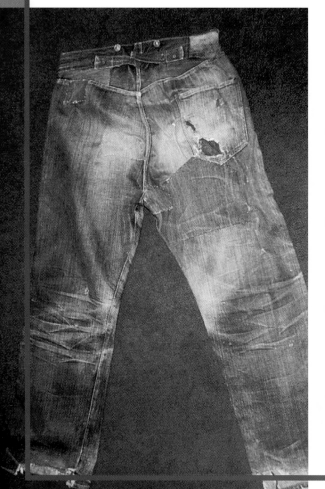

This pair of 501 jeans is more than 100 years old.

This advertisement for Levi Strauss & Co. features different types of clothing, including shirts and overalls.

In the 1800s, many advertisements for Levi Strauss & Co. targeted cowboys.

A Community Man

Levi loved his work. He didn't mind putting in long hours. Levi also enjoyed giving back to his community. He was a generous man. In fact,

The University of California, Berkeley, in the early 1900s

Levi started giving money to **orphanages** before he was wealthy. As he became more successful, he continued to share his wealth with orphanages in California.

Levi also enjoyed helping schools. He gave money to the California School for the Deaf. He also gave college scholarships to the University of California, Berkeley. He set up funds so that even after he died, money would still go to his **charities.**

◄ Levi donated money to many
different orphanages.

21

In addition, Strauss gave his time to worthy causes. He was a religious man and was active in his **synagogue.** He served on the San Francisco Board of Trade and was well respected for his fairness and business sense. He also advised several important companies.

Strauss was known for being an honest businessman. He treated his customers fairly. He had good relationships with the other companies he worked with. His employees were told to call him Levi, never Mr. Strauss. Customers and employees respected him.

A Levi Strauss & Co. store in the 1900s ▶

Levi was also a caring family man. Although he never married, he was very close to his brothers and sisters. He treated his nephews like his own children. As Levi grew older, he let his nephews—Jacob, Sigmund, Louis, and Abraham—help run the business.

Levi Strauss
was a respected
businessman.

Remembering Levi's Life

In the fall of 1902, Strauss began to feel ill. On the evening of September 26, he decided he was well enough to enjoy dinner with his family. Later that night, he died in his home. Newspapers carried the news, and people all over the world were saddened by Levi's death. On the day of his funeral, September 29, businesses throughout San Francisco closed so people could attend the funeral service.

More than 100 years later, Levi Strauss is remembered for his famous blue jeans. He is also remembered for the charities that still receive his support and for the scholarships that are still given out in his name. Always a family man, he would be happy to know that Levi Strauss & Co. is still owned by members of his family.

This display can be seen at the Levi Strauss Museum in Buttenheim.

The Original Levi's Store

A Levi's Store in New York City

Important Dates in Levi Strauss's Life

1829	Born on February 26 in Buttenheim, Bavaria
1847	Immigrates to the United States
1853	Becomes a U.S. citizen; moves to San Francisco and starts his own wholesale company
1863	Names his business Levi Strauss & Co.
1872	Receives a letter from Jacob Davis, who shares the idea of using rivets to reinforce denim pants
1873	Obtains a patent for making riveted denim pants with Jacob Davis
1890	The number 501 is assigned to the original riveted pants
1902	Dies on September 26 at the age of 73

Glossary

charities—organizations that raise money to help people in need

immigrate—to move from one country to live in another

orphanages—places where children without families can live

patent—a legal document that gives an inventor the right to make and produce an item

peddlers—people who sell things by traveling door to door or town to town

rivets—strong metal bolts used to hold things together

synagogue—a place where Jewish people gather and worship

tailor—a person who makes or alters clothing

trademarks—registered symbols used to tell one brand from a competitor's

tuberculosis—a serious bacterial disease that affects the lungs

Did You Know?

- Levi's® jeans were called waist overalls until the 1960s.

- Levi Strauss & Co. uses almost 1.25 million miles (2 million kilometers) of thread each year. That's enough thread to wrap around Earth 50 times!

- In 2001, Levi Strauss & Co. bought back what may be the oldest pair of jeans. The company paid $46,532 to a man who found the jeans buried in a Nevada mining town.

- Today, Levi Strauss & Co. makes 501® jeans in approximately 108 sizes and 20 different fabrics.

- In 1935, Levi Strauss & Co. was the first company to sell blue jeans for women.

Want to Know More?

At the Library

Ford, Carin T. *Levi Strauss: The Man Behind Blue Jeans.* Berkeley Heights, N.J.:
    Enslow Publishers, 2004.

Goldish, Meish. *Levi Strauss: Blue Jean Tycoon.* Vero Beach, Fla.: Rourke, 1993.

Henry, Sondra, and Emily Taitz. *Levi Strauss: Everyone Wears His Name.*
    Minneapolis: Dillon Press, 1990.

Peterson, Tiffany. *Levi Strauss.* Chicago: Heinemann Library, 2003.

On the Web

For more information on *Levi Strauss,* use FactHound
to track down Web sites related to this book.

  1. Go to *www.compasspointbooks.com/facthound*
  2. Type in this book ID: 0756505682
  3. Click on the *Fetch It* button.

Your trusty FactHound will fetch the best Web sites for you!

Through the Mail

Levi Strauss & Co.

Worldwide and U.S. Headquarters

1155 Battery St.

San Francisco, CA 94111

To learn about the Levi Strauss Foundation and its charitable work

On the Road

Levi Strauss Museum

250 Valencia St.

San Francisco, CA 94103

510/210-0110

To visit a working factory and learn more about the history of Levi's® jeans

Index

About the Author

Lucia Raatma received her bachelor's degree in English literature from the University of South Carolina and her master's degree in cinema studies from New York University. She has written a wide range of books for young people. When she is not researching or writing, she enjoys going to movies, practicing yoga, and spending time with her husband, daughter, and golden retriever. She lives in New York.